I WANT TO ELOPE FROM WHERE THERE IS NO
TRADITION INTO A TRADITION

AND THEN OUT AGAIN, THE SWEATY GRIP OF
TRADITION

WINNER OF THE 2013
SAWTOOTH POETRY PRIZE

DAN BEACHY-QUICK, JUDGE

AHSAHTA PRESS
BOISE, IDAHO

2014

PRACTICE
ON
MOUNTAINS

DAVID BARTONE

Ahsahta Press, Boise State University, Boise, Idaho 83725-1525
ahsahtapress.org
Cover design by Quemadura / Book design by Janet Holmes
Printed in Canada

LIBRARY OF CONGRESS CATALOGING-IN-PUBLICATION DATA

Bartone, David.
[Poems. Selections]
Practice on Mountains / David Bartone.
pages cm.——(Sawtooth Poetry Prize)
Includes bibliographical references and index.
Winner of the 2013 Sawtooth Poetry Prize.
ISBN-13: 978-1-934103-47-0 (paperback : alk. paper)
ISBN-10: 1-934103-47-0 (paperback : alk. paper)
I. Title.
PS3602.A77785A6 2014
811'.6—dc23
2013030937

ACKNOWLEDGMENTS

The following sections of the poem, sometimes in various iterations, have been published in these journals, thanks to their editors: "A Way to See the World that Doesn't Need a Jolt: Notes Leading to Translation" in *Aldus: A Journal of Translation*, "Slippage Is a Privilege Theme" in *Thermos Magazine*, and "The Prince's Downfall Involved Li Po in a Second Exile" and "Beekeeping and Hearth-cooking" in *Verse Online*. / Endless debt to the earlier authors of ideas and phrases that have made their way into this work—there are many. / For Jeff Downey and for Zach Savich, for reading and for tireless conversation, thank you—this book has new life because of you. I'd also like to thank Ahsahta Press, Dan Beachy-Quick, Kyle Flak, Janet Holmes, Paul Lisicky, Lisa Olstein, Caryl Pagel, Hilary Plum, Isaac Sullivan, Dara Wier, and my friends and family.

CONTENTS

Another deluge would disgrace mankind.

HENRY DAVID THOREAU

Let me bow my head in labor then, but before I go I will build
here a monument to this new thing, faith, and dedicate it to the
mystery before me that I may look up from my labor when I am
weary and remember how I am thinking now and here.

WILLIAM CARLOS WILLIAMS

Have no twisty thoughts.

SHIH CHING

PROLOGUE. **HERO'S OFFENSES**

I don't write poems that much anymore and so I must apologize if I am unable to express.

I don't write letters that much anymore.

I don't write prayers that much.

We all want to know what's what happens.

. . .

The mercy seat is not as religious bent as bending is a move to make oneself happy, a move to dignity.

To make easy.

3

. . .

Always off just a little bit I have a real solution to love games gone awry you must know.

. . .

Beautiful friend, the motion to dethrone you is meant to raise you up you must know this you must believe me.

. . .

Beautiful friend, you are the reader.

The mercy seat I know is yours alone.

Here I hand it back.

ONE. **MORALITY TO IMPROVE INTO WHICH BY THE WAY IT ROAMS**

She said she'd welcome the debate but don't stop breathing so, she begging breathing.

This was then the new obsession beginning: breathing.

She said you, reader, dear poetry, would say the worst things to me.

She said you're not rubbing the wrong skin you're running me back into my own skin, and I believed her.

That's how wrong you are, you are wrong you know, friend.

Beautiful friend, she said so and I believe her I have to.

The giant her.

Is a real person.

In my real life.

Who may be breaking my heart.

. . .

Breaking my heart sawbucked over yours.

. . .

We use the word *intersection* for everything.

We cook all the time, we never eat.

Our eyes are freshman big.

WE CAN ALWAYS PRETEND NOTHING HAPPENED.

. . .

You and me, beautiful reader.

. . .

The sentimental moment is never satisfied, and there is a reason for this.

It is a literary reason.

The satisfaction moment is a moment within which to reconcile, to reckon with.

I cannot know if I am taking you along.

. . .

This editing forward, calibrating idea back to emotion and emotion into language, always with the next sentence, always forward, comes with a lot of replay affection.

This editing forward is bad advertising for the way the mind works but not bad advice.

THIS IS MY MIND FENDING: the sky is skylit always the way I miss her.

Fending off nothing in particular I would feel comfortable revealing.

Fending off you perhaps, beautiful friend, I'm sorry.

I practically have a therapist in you.

. . .

Beautiful reader.

. . .

I am trying to inhabit you, reader, but I'm sure it seems like I am trying to revile you.

Prepare you.

. . .

I am cute and full of ardor.

This wavers.

. . .

You two are my mistresses.

You are my sacred mistress, and she is my gallivanting mistress, and I don't suppose you two need to compete with each other as much as I need you to feel competitive.

To satisfy me so whole.

If only I can control the outcome, if only I can control everything.

Control from accounting, to check against a duplicate roll for fact, Bartleby the Scrivener, not Bartleby the Controller, for remember his preference to not check his copy work, he is not controlling.

You are my mistresses and I have tried to check you against everything I dwell on.

. . .

My ruminations, my apparitions.

. . .

Comfort, let me say, is not a thing anyone can mean as much as caress.

. . .

She keeps asking why I return to her.

Her clothes are arranged in a pile, she arranges my clothes in a pile.

It's mirth to see as such. Like come have a look-see, a mirth-see.

. . .

We are playing *This is why* once again.

. . .

A sea of reason.

. . .

The sea is a temptable being I know.

The sea is a temperatured being and is eating my leg alive.

(This is an example of flaccid surrealism. It is indifferent surrealism. Hollow and arbitrary, and all too mine. It is an example of flaccid writing. I've always wanted to know what flaccid writing is. I've always wanted. To know what flaccid writing is is flaccid writhing. This I know.) (I am able to understand my quest but unable to discover it. I am able to understand my quest but unable to cease it, which is epic foolishness. It is definitional and foolish. This is what therapists live for. A couples shrink, what is that for. Beautiful paragon, her and I will need such strength. You and I reader will need such strength. To resist then to forfeit resistance. It is but a moment of surrealism, do not apologize. It is a mere moment of surrealism, do nothing. Then move on.)

The mercy seat is not the sea but it can become so if.

The mercy seat is not religious.

This wrecking habit of religion yet again destroying faith.

. . .

How to break from the loop: check the chest, come with that spur.

. . .

The mercy seat, historically speaking, is something on the Ark of the Covenant, it is believed, but unsure of what exactly, and books on it seem meant to cast something mystical about it too, but mystical about it or it being unknown, I can't tell.

Be night traveling until you know.

Anything.

. . .

I have been in affair with a married woman for eight months.

It is October 13, 2010.

I do not feel entitled to my emotions.

. . .

I question my lyrical faith.

I question everything.

. . .

And I believe her.

. . .

Mirth is the surface, joy is the happiness internal.

The theory developed inside and I felt ashamed to admit its faulty logic worked.

The theory I confess.

The theory I confess is not mine it is Kyle's a friend working for years before as a security guard at the Bissell vacuum cleaner factory near Grand Rapids, Michigan, and devoted himself to the theory's attention.

The theory that mirth is the surface joy.

The theory that mirth is the surface joy is the happiness internal.

. . .

On February 12 I walked with the married girl I loved and told her I cannot lug her carelessness out of her but believe me I try, I was writing one million sonnets in one hand cracking a walnut in the other.

It is not impossible to know like this.

Still.

Stillness of the now-preservable, and aching, but don't preserve it, and don't ache it, it is not your work, and it is not my work, it is not my work.

. . .

To a whole home god celeste assure.

Fly fly fly away in the morning.

When I die away hallelujah by and by.

When the shadows on this life I roam.

Fly away fly fly away.

Like a bird to a prison bird, fly away old glory in the morning.

Hallelujah by and by to a bird.

. . .

Just a few more weary days and days to a land where New Jersey never ends I fly away.

. . .

Enter again the etcetera moment.

. . .

I don't write poems that much anymore and there is anxiety for this or that that can go off.

If you are not careful.

Tonight it is poems and cement.

Tonight poems and tidal notions.

Tonight poems and undertow.

Tonight poems. Put on notice the portion of your self left on the peel.

Tonight poems and ideas of faith, faith and control, ideas of forfeiting, the idea that at thirty you are sleeping until three in the afternoon waking muttering "whatever happens I'll be okay whatever happens I'll be okay" and reading then Shakespeare's histories for Christ's sake, King John, *The Life and Death of King John*.

Complete but wholly inept a name, the life and death of a minded thing compels me.

Something unseen carrying Shakespeare through the writing of the histories.

Me and you, beautiful friend, do that for him, we are the readers.

The something unseen carrying him.

. . .

I am trying to behave entirely self *left*.

Vanity in trying anything self at all, vanity tries anything at all.

And I hope you will forgive me of the slick intractable bond I make between us born of vanity.

. . .

Isaac believes leaning back in his chair as if leaning forward that I must let myself experience the heartbreak.

Zach believes I can have the worst month of my life, and be still.

Jeff says, sir, timing.

It is practically a difficulty to hear this from them, though they are right now right.

. . .

What's worth most?

The worth must be telling.

. . .

The study of a sentence is about.

Sentence and sentiment from the same, to be of the opinion of, to ope.

To ape a dead poet.

. . .

One thing I cannot explain is how students seem to use the word *delve* to mean anything they think when they are holding a book, they call reading *delving*.

What to give them?

The sword tonight?

How gestural.

No, chart every thought tonight, notebooks cut quick into full immediate form, less the melody if the melody carries strain, less the freight if it has too much matter, less the spirit if it hasn't a ghost, less the kiss if it hasn't a shadow, chart the rest well, chart the well, rest, understand if you may.

I question my rambling faith.

I question the sword tonight but I don't question falling and flying.

. . .

High altitude geese migration above, I cannot hear them, I can seem them.

. . .

Let me be clear, for those near.

I know where to seek for the shape of things I cannot see.

Zach knows how to pattern his eye after what he is seeing, he is a better poet than me.

Jeff has trajectory always in mind, taking orbit as verb not path, he is a better poet than me.

Kyle has joy when he goes for walks and I try to tell him it is about having his breathing regulated, the way that a poem can do for you, sometimes he has no reaction at all to the things I say, the mirth-joy theory is his, he is a better poet than me.

I do not give Jeff enough credit when I am interpreting his kind posture as nervous posture, he is a better poet than me. We are in Panera Bread and he is a newlywed and I am talking frivolously about love affairs, and I get worse at who I am.

Hilary doesn't tell jokes one too many times, she is a better poet than me, she is a better person than me.

. . .

Do I myself believe I will ever narrate for you what is going on
in my life.

What seems to pit you, beautiful friend, beautiful reader,
against her in me.

Do I myself not believe in what's prenatal.

. . .

I am scared to admit this: the river is partial, from any view,
except from in it.

. . .

Yes it seems we are all looking for heaven on earth.

In heaven, it is my belief, you get to choose which tense of life
verbs occur in.

But the belief never lasts and I do not consider myself faithful.

. . .

You can say this is baptismal.

. . .

The grand lyrical gesture is not in the absence of metaphor, and it is not in the metaphor itself.

It is simple and in the transfer of a sound into a looser sound.

Sound here can mean many things.

It can mean sturdiness, of course, or the *allargando*, the broadening.

. . .

Do not call similes dumb, you would not believe their teeth.

Teeth so crisp, teeth so blunt.

Bone on bone, like sitting in a bathtub, every bone that touches the tub.

. . .

Longwinded or blunt.

. . .

Amazing the things that do and do not need to be said.

What is this *it* everyone's talking about, the importance of *coming to it*.

. . .

It originally that she is able to overcome her cravings and I am not.

. . .

I would like to say to you there is no way I can repay you, friend, for listening to this me, this long.

I would like to say that is my favorite part about poetry, I cannot repay you.

I would like to say to you I am not, I know, an immediacy to reckon with, I would like, I'm not anything to reckon with, which I mean: I am tired love and even scared of charting the places my mind wanders when I am thinking of this life I live without you, beautiful reader.

I would like to say to you I am searching for a faith.

I am aware that useless if you have to ask exists, and therefore useless if you have to tell exists.

Perhaps this is coming out churlish and masked.

Perhaps this will change into something we can come to love.

This living without.

This living will.

. . .

Stretching my arm I stretch the other arm and live a long way away.

. . .

I have seen the poem both ways.

Even in Kyoto, how I long for old Kyoto when the cuckoo sings.

And with lyricism an emphasis falls on longing:

When in Kyoto—
hearing the cuckoo retch—
I long for Kyoto.

—Basho

. . .

It is important to carve out a space for your morality to improve into which by the way it roams.

It roams by fire.

Baptism by fire.

By invasion.

By baptism.

By *bildungsroman*.

The first becoming of Christ.

. . .

By tempt or by temper.

This I must know.

. . .

I have seen the poem this way.

"Tell General Howard I know his heart," said Chief Joseph.

. . .

If I truly accept the heartache I would not need to hate her, I could live so close to her and let her go.

A balloon almost touching the ground.

I confess the process must be beautiful.

Or the swallows in my heart stain phantom sized and fearful.

Or phantom sized and cornered.

Phantom sized and confessed.

Phantom sized and my hand (here I am the priest) covering her mouth.

She has just left my booth.

The fastest way to clear her name is to divulge what I know.

I cannot do that I confess.

That if you turn around and see me crying you do not have to proceed with your plan to come to me (or to not), friend, I am phantom sized about this and inconsolable.

From time to time.

Hand to hand and booth to booth, I confess beautiful friend.

I confess you quietly.

Introduce the concept that in the end you might be right.

I confess you with the bellows.

I confess you from one end of the room to the other.

. . .

It is October 15, and I am getting grand.

I do not feel entitled to my emotions but in the last twenty-four hours at some point I have.

This indicates the baptismal space but gives no method for filling it.

I criticize the baptismal space.

. . .

Criticism in excess of poetry.

Poetry in excess of life.

From despair it becomes easy in life to assert what is necessary.

To write a sentence that cannot possibly withstand the closest reading in the most given context.

Okay.

I mean a sentence by Melville, a term, this being of the opinion of, a true and Latin sentence.

Acrobatics beheld.

Beholding sentiment.

To write a sentence that finally captures everything that was so penetrably and impenetrably teeming in the last three to five years of one's own poetry.

The thing that could not fit.

I realize poetry has been practice on mountains.

And there is no longing anymore to do.

I pick a poem I would only read you if I had one minute to read to you, and it does not fit.

I am as earnest as Robert Frost.

I am trying to make it fit, I am going for legacy.

I do not know other models for this.

. . .

I do not know if I have made my point clear and so I know I
have begun a new middle.

Suggestion of more to come.

. . .

A noose middled.

. . .

I regret to accept a psychological truth to the lyric.

To have to accept.

. . .

Isaac sent me a poem today and from it "I'm coming this short of
saying / yes, but I want to say yes"

He knows tonight I am immobility full of song.

I am resisting calling upon her with the full song semantic of my full sung body from my full song mouth to her ear.

. . .

The way her eyes come down, she presses two fingers under her ear and tilts her head, a stress ache, she pays this attention to her body.

. . .

And from the poem at A to the resistance my body bears, B, the entire attachments are mine to make.

. . .

I am here the beautiful friend.

. . .

Tonight: yes, but I want to say yes.

Tonight: the will to do as you do, the guide, the Beatrice, the Guido.

Tonight the mountains.

Tonight the mountains I would forfeit to call upon her.

Amazing the things I strive to forfeit.

Amazing the things that do and do not need to be done to move me to immorality.

Amazing the things.

. . .

The most generative things, somehow more meaningful than meaning.

This is faith, at its least, the thing other things rely on.

This is the thing I am always trying to teach myself: faith.

Duty bound and maintaining what's spry, inasmuch as the great circling continues, it is necessary to loosen the sensibilities.

Play, prayer, and orbiting are the yield, not the mode alone.

The teaching that can be named.

The curse.

The cursing continues circling.

. . .

She needs to see if she can live without me.

Her lone prompt.

I can only accept as a literary prompt, to declare, to avow.

. . .

When do you believe me most.

Do you believe me most if I cannot believe it myself.

. . .

I am preparing a bath to remind myself of dying in a bath.

Knowing it is happening is not enough shame to move to prevent the thought.

Self-pity is too much shame.

Body parts like hard casts over shame.

Posture points.

I am at a plot point of loss that seems inevitable and, worse, expected.

. . .

Affairs don't seem freighted from the beginning.

However, there are no previous narratives to prove this for me.

There are no previous narratives for this to prove me.

. . .

Almost reaching to touch the water, touched by glassy steam
from under the crest's collar, Hart was Crane's mother's maiden
name.

As if it was her leaping from the ship, his mother—or permit
her here as a symbol!—who before him took up these tendencies
and first communicated them in him, the wet grip of genetics.

. . .

Causing to deep breathing.

The bathtub scene is the daily ritual but in it I cannot find the
rite.

The part of me that puts one foot in the water and looks at the
hairs on my chest and the hairs on my stomach, and around my
penis, and on my leg.

31

The part of me that can recall doing this all my life.

I am alive because of the part of me that can picture, I must believe this.

That can invoke.

The pool or the mud pool or the bathtub the night before.

Bones thirty years old in the daily bath, no thing brittle, no thing supple.

. . .

"Second becoming" complex, beginning.

. . .

I cannot begin to chart the shames, apart from: the shame I feel most compelled to tell you about is the shame that, you and me, beautiful friend, our relationship has moved into a literary therapy, and for this we may be slain a memoir.

So.

Literary shame is the most compelling shame.

Because it is the most confounding?

Because it is the most mustered in me.

. . .

The sea is the image, the sea is the rising I am most often.

The sea is me taking too much kindness in myself.

The snow at sea that flails falls on it eventually.

The rain at sea that ripens it rips it open.

New gashes in the surface tension.

The etcetera continues.

The however is ceaseless.

The against moment only outweighed by the again moment.

It is unclear whether that is a good thing.

. . .

Wanting her to know when it becomes clear to her that her
husband cannot forgive her she should look for me my bidding
still binding.

. . .

Disgust with the calendar.

Disgust with the evergreens disguised as evergreens.

Time and needles taking time to turn brown.

. . .

You will have to forgive me if for several pages this hasn't involved you.

As ever: the aphorism buried in the apology is yet working to lift itself.

. . .

Self-righteousness abounds first from hearsay play.

See: heresy.

Phantom sized and real, I don't read the Bible.

Phantom sized and real, she doesn't read the Bible.

We read the other ground, phantom sized and real.

Ion and the muse, assure me.

Symposium, assure me.

Augustine of Hippo, assure me.

Dante and Cervantes. Shelley and Byron.

This list wouldn't end but would if it did with a simple proof that every word carries the meaning of each other word, it would list every literature until it had listed every word, the way that lexicographers choose how many alternate definitions for a word to print but don't choose how many exist, every word also means its opposite because of this.

Arriving at graspable infinity.

Tending toward, as *what* approaches.

Her no.

. . .

I'm going to keep on.

. . .

Timing is everything, when there is bad timing there must be faith.

When there is a bad intersection, there must be faith then.

Or a longer love affair.

And hoards of non-herding tropes.

Everlasting in reach.

Or a stoma stretching in the bowel.

When there's a stand-in for faith, faith.

Or the anaphoric mind eight months too dwelling, roll with that.

. . .

I'm going to keep on climbing it's true.

Gradations and ingratiations.

I'm going to empty the nest it's true.

. . .

It is October 18, and I called her today and could it possibly matter.

. . .

You beautiful reader have been patient and forgive me if I haven't thrown you a few regarded or necessary pages here and there, I wanted never to condescend.

. . .

Formidable three, you me and her, how can we ever get along.

. . .

Even I even out even now.

TWO. **CLOSENESS A TERRIBLE DISTANCE**

Eroticism and purgatory linger in me the wasted faiths.

On one hand, on the other.

The overlap: vivid the thoughts at night that pulse toward her crawling in bed at night from the bottom.

At night with the thought.

Bringing her knee full to her chest, this is full crawling.

Every beautiful thought comes tinctured with a caress now jealous.

Jealous not of who would attract her, the grass to the cow, the cosmos to the bumblebee, but of those who have her and would deject her, the farmer, the bumblebee curled frost dead this morning in the whitish pink cosmos.

It is not me in bed every night that she is arriving.

It is October 20, and I feel entitled to a room of her apparition stroking along the haunt.

. . .

For a little while longer, I will perform like this: taking hold in me a room full of tables and the sprawl of books and the scatter of papers, this winter to overwinter, this timber to fell.

And I will wait to see what comes next.

. . .

I have always wanted to believe that I had somehow always given you, beautiful friend, beautiful reader, a certain grace that says we are aligned, I believe in you, or something to that effect.

Same page syndrome.

. . .

I have always believed in special effects, and have wanted to.

To believe not that they should premiere in a relationship but that they do occur at all is enough and titillating.

And now I am done with that conviction.

They should premiere because they can.

. . .

The musical score of our lives takes precedence, in romance and in action and in dramatic courage, etcetera, and that that precedence of music-driven movement would lead her to me, her in her lip biting or her in her tongue pressing behind her top two teeth the way she does when she, say, is wearing jeans to the office on her day off, her errand day, and you don't know her yet, you flirt with her, these of her, moments you couldn't possibly need me to picture, now or ever, don't you, beautiful friend, have anything to draw from, I hope so, I place hope in so, I am displaced if not so.

I accept then also.

I am reaching for her and taking my epistolary energy into new patiences, not for loving her but for living of her, is to say: without her.

. . .

Beyonce is her name.

The farmer tells me, walking toward me with a new measure in his eye, then turning away to do anything else.

I am holding my nephew two feet from the electric fence, he is squirmy, reaching for the cow—her big beautiful eyes.

. . .

Did you know I have never touched these cows, I am so close to them.

Did you know I have never touched a horse, I don't want to use up the experience.

There is sadness—a certain melancholy—to reading up everything by your favorite author.

Love the author, though it is a one-way love to bathe in, lay naked in refuse, tidy up the laundry pile somehow, begin in on someone else's lifework, and don't you dare be careful about it.

. . .

Beautiful friend, reader, you and her are my mistresses.

Perhaps if I disdain you this is why, beautiful friend, you are the sacred fool, and if I her, for being spineless and gallivanting.

. . .

With you, friend, I never wanted to consummate the affair, I only ever wanted it to feel like spring.

. . .

I fear you only read me.

I am one psycho-lithic presumption after another, my mind turned to stone, then to another stone.

And I fear you treat me like it.

. . .

Her, she called me yesterday and we talked about moving into friendship, a then seeming reasonable request.

Friendship, her failure of spine, not love, she says.

. . .

Close, I have never been closer to someone in my life.

And I mean this from the perspective of loving.

Closeness a terrible distance, it means no touching.

I am talking about her, I am talking about you too, beautiful friend, beautiful reader.

THREE. **THE PRINCE'S DOWNFALL INVOLVED LI PO IN A SECOND EXILE**

The trouble with being good at courting patrons.

The prince's downfall involved Li Po in a second exile, though they spoke of it an excursion.

. . .

The fall has now entered fog fall as a way to help Li Po understand himself, which he accepts.

He'll be back by Indian summer.

. . .

Exile: drink, write nothing until Indian summer.

The energy of his thighs enough to carry him.

. . .

Attention wolf fans:

Indian summer has already garnered tons of praise and will
arrive just in time for Halloween.

. . .

It has been thus far a four-colored fall.

Kitchen window light. Stove light. Sink light. Lamp.

. . .

Spry sprung into a full force of passion, lovers obey this time of
year approaching with their ears to the leaf crinkle.

Old lovers leave-taking in old friends.

. . .

To see through the thick now, sense of a band playing down low
over the hill.

This, the prince's downfall: always sensing down low over the
hill.

FOUR. QUIXOTE IN THE BEDROOM

The sixteenth century collapsed into one bronze Don Quixote
around the corner.

He so immersed himself in those romances that he spent whole
days and nights over his books.

Permit me be bold in these ways. Permit me some knight-
errantry. Permit me harvest eyes like two folding moons.

I want to make classic beauty, to elope into it.

Elope from the sixteenth century French, abscond, run away.
But before that from the Norman Anglican, to leap.

I want to elope from where there is no tradition into a tradition
and then out again, the sweaty grip of tradition.

There is no wandering in search of chivalrous adventures for me.

There is the dim lit home collapsing all space between two people like two folding moons sitting in opposite chairs like two opposite rooms.

. . .

Is all.

. . .

I have never been very good at describing the ways my lover touches me.

There seems no act that more exaggerates the insufficiencies of both lyricism and realism.

I have tried to narrate her motion her eyes her face, but searching, I find alone snapshots that are alone and by the way and in third person.

The gross move that occurs in literature, the desperate default of third person.

I finally said it.

. . .

She brings one knee up to her chest. A little.

I bill and coo.

FIVE. **A WAY TO SEE THE WORLD THAT DOESN'T NEED A JOLT: NOTES LEADING TO TRANSLATION**

A way into the plunge that doesn't need a jolt.

A way home.

A way, a migration from the plains, a calm migration from the plains.

Plain put, a way that is not wayward.

And a ward that is not stationary.

A way out from the tidiest autumn, into say hard frost, which this year occurs first after Indian summer, and a way out from that.

A double-bolted door. On the side with the bolt switches.

A way a common flower with a disease dies out, bumblebees die out.

The way the farmer's wit next door in the form of his low laugh, the way to know his newly killed cow, his screaming at his child, daily, and there's nothing to do about it.

The farmer's wit next door collapsing in on itself. By some moral presumption I have over him.

He is shirtless and it is cold and I am indoors.

Am searching for a way into pleasure not wit, then; not righteousness either—to be very careful of that.

The couch has wit, unnatural wit, be careful of that. Do not get up.

The couch, it has patterned pink globe peonies and blue dyed mums.

The couch has haiku.

. . .

The practicing on mountains is not as obsessed with you, beautiful friend, beautiful reader, as it has claimed.

Her neither.

. . .

To defy the couch is highest.

. . .

I have placed my bed so that the sun will wake me at 7:45 am. It is October 30.

The autumn sunrise. The bed is a page.

A way to remember the close of summer as an elegant conclusion.

The last swim a swim in colors.

The sun high up, in summer, and therefore not coming in on the bed, then, in former summer—when each lunch spent with her and smells of butter and her smells filled the room and my skin.

I could taste myself on her neck.

I mean in saying this to be careful for not to be too much of a jolt.

See the world. From the world.

Now low, the autumn sunrise, and a streaking through the branches.

I can see from the window the ripe berries of the horse nettle, and the sight draws me to move myself outdoors, but I stay in bed where the sun is more mine.

. . .

It is in this way, too, I believe in language manipulation: one can always live more on a page.

The abandoned branches between and the low morning sun— the essay—of every word.

Essential, be, ascertain, trial. All from the same, in Latin. This to me is the archeology of the human mind at its most fascinating.

The fascination of the human mind is that certain action occurring off scene is made more vivid because of, and certain action occurring off scene is stress-inducing. For years people have called this *abstract v concrete.* For centuries people have called that *Hellenic dramatic action v Shakespearean.*

The fascination is *this* scene, not what happened on or off of it in between this and the last. Or this and the next.

It is in this fascination I most implicate you, reader. You are here with me. For or against will.

We are here.

. . .

My love occurs both on and off stage, as it may.

. . .

There is a low body, laughing in its huge past. And it is not the farmer's.

There is a low body silenced, out outright of its own fortune. And it is not the farmer's.

The body crowing alone, as the poetics of the mind become far off and fully into themselves.

. . .

The problem with what to call the body after it has departed this present is a delicate one.

Body corpse remains carcass cadaver. These are crass.

What if when how the body is what's departed, then shall we call what remains the departed? The soul?

. . .

This is an example of the inevitable fray to babble, when the body drifts but the mind remains on the couch.

In this sense I am still gazing out the window and the tone of haiku is losing its effect on me.

. . .

Once again the tone has been exhausted before the form has.

. . .

Not a bad understanding of the twentieth century.

. . .

However the fear then, to think this way, in what to write next.

Is all of writing avoiding fear of what not to.

. . .

How many, afraid of trope and cliché. How many.

. . .

And I may mean saying this, now, is appropriate to say: As I
am getting older I find myself searching less for a way to justify
my arrogance, my shame shrinks, and I am becoming a better
person.

Which is true.

And I wonder if not for all of us.

. . .

I am searching for a way to see the world that doesn't need a
jolt.

I am searching for the writer as translator, when translating.

A jolt, sure, the writer who translates, in the aim of bringing a
new literature into an extant literature.

But not a jolt, when in the act of translating.

. . .

What do you think Pound meant when he said the poet should
write 75 lines of poetry a day, and since a young poet can't
possibly have 75 lines of poetry to write each day, the poet

should learn a language and translate 75 lines a day.

. . .

He meant: The macro of purposes for committing a translation into your language is not now a measure of one's love of language, but of merging.

A sympathetic but proud endeavor.

To merge importances.

One's with yours.

. . .

I am trying to be sympathetic but not proud in trying to separate you, beautiful friend, from her, my love.

Here I am meant to say it: I am ashamed, of myself, and while not of Pound, of poetry, for creating this sentiment in him, the cynical cliff we teeter toward.

I accept and embrace his hubris.

. . .

I am not literate in any foreign languages.

I am ashamed before this.

When I hear that Pound once said the poet should write 75 lines, I sometimes wish I had more friends that speak foreign languages.

And would that count.

And why in the way that I find relationships meaningful do I think yes.

. . .

The mutually inclusive life with another is one to practice on mountains for.

. . .

I am simple, and thin, I know, and I do not mean only about my relationship to English.

I mean: shameful, about all language, of the facts, to be an assertion of my belief or of my self in any way, but simply the need to speak plainly about the linguistic makeup of my character—as a way to, perhaps, understand my own poetic intelligence pressed against peaceable notions of shame.

Poetic intelligence and notions of shame. The two go on co-
conquering.

. . .

Pound must have meant: Do not get up.

. . .

I obey in this certain way: I make more psycho-lithography from
the couch and accept becoming my own faith.

. . .

More than this psycho-lithography from the couch.

I make a poetic activity of Pound's of Li Po's, translations of poems.

. . .

Give me that old time religion, a little brown church in the dale.

. . .

Do I condemn everything I believe by saying translation is a poetic
activity and not a scholastic one, very well then, I am large, I
contain.

This is a truly confessionalist tenet: to mean it now. This is a truly surrealist tenet: to mean it now. This is a truly pathetic tenet;—it is truly transferable across all genres.

. . .

The title is Pound's. The formal shape of the poem on the page is Pound's. Some phrases and entire lines are Pound's; the epigraph is his. The poetics are more mine, not Li Po's, not Pound's. Note, if you do, the homophonic interpretations. Note: they are sounded to thin-align with my own emotional narratives:

LEAVE-TAKING NEAR SHOKU
'Sanso, King of Shoku, built roads'

Thistles roar in sand sores on the feet.
Fear as the dismount ends.
The walls rise in a man's face.
Blouses flow out from the sill
      as his coarse bride dies in him.
Weepingly, anon, separation offers begin in him.
The air's unkind bruise, the separation,
And freshets are bursting their ice.
      In the missive she cooed a scarcity:

"Man faces hours of faulty steps,
There is no kneeling off, we kingly lovers."

And:

TAKING LEAVE OF A FRIEND

Bloom out and storm through them alms.
Why strive her? Why *thing about* then?
Here we must make separation
And goad through Athens. And why lessen the grass?
Mine lies a calf, loading white cloud.
Son, settle. Because the part we dug weighted fences,
That now of her hair clasp, what a pittance.
Of course, to pray to hug her,
a sway art of parting.

And:

THE JEWEL STAIRS' GRIEVANCE

To choose and pep the oral eddies—quite a wait without
    you—
It is to wait that, without you so, keeps my cause of talking.
In my bed, I drown in the crisscross patterns,
And watch the moon through the clear autumn.

And this one, which was enjoyable to write but occurs to me
to be an unsatisfying textual account of the poem's musical
potential; the boisterous wit of the compound words, too,
is a distraction from the common fact that to a stranger in a
challenging land, art might get them their ward:

SOUTH-FOLK IN COLD COUNTRY

Today's course nasal-gets the plea, going *It's you!*
The words of *It's you!* half-annul the offer. Enter forth,
Emotion is born out of habit.
Yes, to straying-bent touting the gilded fool's fate.
To stray from the drag of the pen.
Her prized dessert to her male season.
Lying below the wilderness the barbs are in feathers.
My sworn ilk pants of her hour's acute presence.
My ended-spear odd-arrived at other heavenly banners.
Art might get him his ward.
Solely my art tax is mine.
Honeybees are left for me if she goes,
       this whiff hovering.
Whose white head is lost for this province?

SIX. **BEEKEEPING AND HEARTH-COOKING**

Consider what Thoreau proposes:

"There are certain pursuits which, if not wholly poetic and true, do at least suggest a nobler and finer relation to nature than we know. The keeping of bees, for instance, is a very slight interference. It is like directing the sunbeams. All nations, from the remotest antiquity, have thus fingered nature. There are Hymettus and Hybla, and how many bee-renowned spots beside! There is nothing gross in the idea of these little herds—their hum like the faintest low of kine in the meads. A pleasant reviewer has lately reminded us that in some places they are led out to pasture where the flowers are most abundant. 'Columella tells us,' says he, 'that the inhabitants of Arabia sent their hives into Attica to benefit by the later-blowing flowers.' Annually are the hives, in immense pyramids, carried up the Nile in boats, and suffered to float slowly down the stream by night, resting by day, as the flowers put forth along the banks; and they determine the richness of any locality, and so the profitableness of delay, by the sinking of the boat in the water. We are told, by the same reviewer, of a man in Germany, whose bees yielded more honey than those of his neighbors, with no apparent advantage; but at length he informed them, that he had turned his hives one degree more to the east, and so his bees, having two hours the start in the morning, got the first sip of honey. True, there is treachery and selfishness behind all this, but these things suggest to the poetic mind what might be done."

. . .

During the Q & A portion with experts on Lydia Maria Child, an audience member tries to sell one of the speakers a $125 library licensed video on Lydia Maria Child, and as though I could be a community college professor for the rest of my life, long long past retirement age, a minor tangle begins up in me, that I must understand as a certain dying of youthful ambition—the sentiment I could write anything, not gone but going.

. ∴ .

Consider a recipe from *The American Frugal Housewife*.

A task to divest oneself then from worldly gods, the game of surviving bettered.

On election day, eat election bread. And so forth the advantages are such.

. . .

The Childs didn't have any children, were abolitionists.

They were poor sugar beet farmers for a time.

He took up the last dollars on a ship ticket to France to learn how to raise sugar beets in central Massachusetts. She remained to raise the sugar beets in central Massachusetts.

The abolitionist movement had come this far: beets not cane then in the North.

. . .

Later in a barroom the kingship is abandoned.

. . .

Today now all this time passes.

. . .

Today now as ever.

. . .

The sum of exiles, greater than Christ and the meek—the mind
making Emily Dickinson of the Old Testament.

. . .

Not wanting to leave myself behind on any worried walk
inward, I decide to step outside of myself for a few days.
I read six poems in *The New York Times*, six poems to mark the
end of daylight savings.

What the Pulitzer Prize winners have.

. . .

Couch in the basement.

SEVEN. **TO BE PRINTED AS IT IS**

The essay on the ellipsis, the poet's need to justify the form.

. . .

The struggle of the first part of life is to distinguish two things,
fault from form.

It seems.

That to comprehend the strength of form is the forte of life.

To provide self-ultimatum of I either change or I don't.

The art of recklessness or I don't.

In the wake of touch, the prod of bounty. Or I don't.

. . .

That, and the struggle of the second part is to envy the second part.

The second part a part that exceeds one's will to make distinctions—I pray.

I want to be old and see everything the same.

. . .

There is no need for students to talk of age just because they are interested in wisdom.

. . .

I am not the forest about this, tough as I am.

. . .

Yeats saying of Blake, saying the limitations of his view come from the very intensity of his vision, saying to hush boy and see the soothe occurring before you.

. . .

I cannot believe I am interested in this method of speaking:
'fort' from form, forlorn before forte's forest forgets.

I cannot believe I do not know anymore if I am dragging you,
beautiful reader, through to me or away. (Or that I ever believed
I did.)

. . .

Pride in the ambulatory nature of pacing, a sure precursor to
reclusion.

However: cloistering not reclusion is the goal, and the difference
is absolute.

. . .

Long before the goal of cloistering ripens in a person, unspoken
inevitable etymology begins.

The cloister was an architectural covering of the monastery's
walkway.

Then: *He took to* the cloister *more than the sword.*

This goes on, the etcetera behavior of language.

. . .

Here out, I do not know if I am addressing myself or if I am addressing you, reader.

However I know the form at hand, of making ellipses as of each erased thought between, is intended to propel my own ease, which is I know a momentary feature, not rest, which is surely more perpetual.

For rest having the most concrete biological effects.

. . .

Ease for both of us, that I get to erase the parts (I erase immediately) that do not threaten to embarrass myself, that you get to (should you choose) read as vertically as you.

Read up and down.

. . .

I am not threatened by excerptibility.

. . .

I am lately inclined to call the general process psycho-lithography, as I have—however, less 'the mind, one stone at a time' and more as 'stones alone, turning into stone' is meant.

I mean: what notes you would find on the posthumous collection of your own miscellany.

What stones you turn over in the flailing first moments of turning to stone.

And of course: what happens to the little poem when I decide to indulge desperation.

I didn't want to say Pompeii.

. . .

This book should have a preface.

It should say it is okay when you want in bed to listen to Debussy.

It should say it is okay to turn the little book you bought to its original ambition, the bed stand.

. . .

It should say this is not a necessarily dogged form of poetry but uncanny in its nonetheless-persistent upheaval.

It should say persistent fortune is actual fortune.

It should back off from time to time and give way for more critical occasion.

It should not.

EIGHT. **SLIPPAGE IS A PRIVILEGE THEME**

The low hollow-like note that indicates the size of the stone.

. . .

The bridegroom's stone, the widower's stone, the pseudo-scientific stone, the nature writer's stone, the *á outrance* stone.

. . .

I, the sub-sub librarian of the stone.

The stone merchant, who leaves no stone unthrown.

. . .

The one scene that navigates all the literary impulses back to it is, I would have you believe now, not made of stone, but a billowy gray day filled with quacking gray flecks.

About one year ago. Like a Beatrice moment.

. . .

Strange how, briefly but frequently, I then for months believed I did not have the ability to focus on one line at a time.

Strange I believed I could not write at all if the epic stroke wasn't in each stroke.

. . .

And this is a good thought if it lingers, for it points ambition upward as well as out.

. . .

That I was taking in too much on the walks to the pond with her last November when the geese when the pond when the cool on the marble bench made us think of each other naked and single and oh how exact our ages to our desires: all thoughts, all perfections.

. . .

This is the closest I will come, in this manner, to narrating the scene.

That you may extinguish hope of finding parable or symbol in some thing that has gripped me because it is now gone and all we have here together is this one pet on this short lead.

. . .

A new name for faith: trust that to wander along would be enough to satisfy.

. . .

The thin spare between calm claim and calamity.

. . .

Given the relief of her company to what I had considered much damage of prior solitude, strange how boldly and with half humor, half pity, I performed all of my tasks.

I perfumed at any task I was handed, and called it flirt.

. . .

Call this that ancient want, that old-time anxiety.

. . .

The self-contradiction man permits upon such aesthetic
pleasures.

. . .

As if charitable at last, it took months at first to realize: I could
not stop writing the scene.

. . .

I could not stop the V to the geese.

Forthrightness to the one disobedient.

Salt to his style, to the renegade.

Longing to the migrant.

. . .

Days pass and I'm still writing the scene. Months of it appearing
to me.

. . .

An American Revolution to a war historian.

. . .

Thoreau to Gandhi.

. . .

Students ask ceaselessly about the ceaseless nature of language
and they do it in phrasings they are comfortable with.

How often do you have to write to be great at it?

I believe it is important to answer the question with a response
that is true.

. . .

As ever, I always am when answering avoiding the emptiest
thought I have.

This I call the truth.

. . .

I call it also dignity and can afford at least this much of it: that if
I don't mean what I say when I say it, I will mean it later when I
am alone, or recounting the events of the conversation to a lover.

. . .

When I am alone I am repossessing the second best thought I could be having, as when with a lover.

The best thought is off somewhere, dragging on the stitch of another long skirt, this is called longing and is what the poet is most practiced at.

. . .

I hymn what I am aware of.

. . .

Do you have to believe in or just be vulnerable to, to make a good poem?

. . .

I hymn them for their singing.

I hymn them for preserving, for the upcoming exhibition.

For being shoal shored.

. . .

I hymn about and feel therefore grounded.

. . .

My house was always dark and empty growing up (—by this upbringing, entirely average), now I write one poem per day, at sunrise or sunset, most often, and it doesn't seem to matter which, or what I write.

. . .

Like scheduled insulin shots into dad's belly.

. . .

By this upbringing, I have always understood the V to the geese.

. . .

This is a true response.

. . .

Though without being asked I could not have felt compelled to assert it.

But this, the cause to assertion, is not what the students are ceaselessly interested in.

. . .

I therefore wonder where my interests are going with them, therefore remember.

. . .

I answer questions with a pause, they know all of my tricks by now.

It is November 17.

The point in the semester where by now we have terrific rapport.

. . .

The point they all point to the laughter moment in every teachable moment, and having perhaps dumbly encouraged it for two months, I am now beginning to show my discomfort with their mirth, I invent an obnoxious assignment for them to perform, the most beautiful person in the room is the one who seems to notice what I'm up to, I am always surprised to discover who it is this time.

. . .

This too is how love's fallen into.

. . .

The person that is most looking at you.

. . .

This in the affair is what compels me to make love to her
pinning to a brick building at dusk on campus.

That she is looking at me.

. . .

How can you refuse him now, I say to the student who couldn't
do the reading last night, the Sonnets.

Because he found out his girlfriend had cheated on him.

(I am becoming *this* teacher.)

No no you don't understand. With my roommate.

(I too know how to teach his way out of this, I tell him.)

You don't understand. *In my bed.*

(It was good when the world was on fire, I say to him.) (But at
this I am losing him, his scorn eyes are now fixed away from
me on nothing or on some happy campus couple walking in the
direction of the dining hall.)

. . .

He asks why we always end up walking out of the classroom
together.

I tell him how bees swarm up for fear of becoming sediment.

He offers me his daily cigarette. I do not.

. . .

One of these days he will sense the mourning period coming to
a close.

. . .

I must say thinking about it now I am becoming very attracted
to his girlfriend I've never met.

. . .

I am slipping into this old self.

This old self we lug around with the pride of genetic banner.

Slippage the privilege.

I am slipping the pride of banter into this old self.

. . .

The reasons for this, upon closer inspection, are not readily available.

. . .

In the desperate clasp, the sweaty hold on the telephone, the sweaty waiting for.

I am shy here to accept that I am still without meaningful faith.

. . .

The elevation of song: I hymn to him.

And the reasons for her departure will be made a bit more available.

. . .

The Ohio soil of speech, and his voice is like a little brown church's bell.

But the reasons she left stay too sealed from him.

. . .

Remembering the still backyards and listening to an ex-lover's family speak about community colleges and the rotary club, etcetera; I thought of a paradise constructed.

. . .

Though this is not paradise made more available, the fair homestead.

I accept it as a construction, therefore a clue.

. . .

Discreet pride in driving past the megachurches.

. . .

Slipping from the pursuit, (which I have better before been able to name than now, I admit.)

This the privilege.

. . .

Slipping from the pursuit, and I want to call it digression, but it seems more stationary than that.

I want to call it beginning but it feels less like a point is coming.

. . .

What if all I do is write the prologue to the epic.

What if the note I sense never satisfies the pre-inhalation.

What if the ever-expanding lung capacity continues and I don't.

What if anxiety and modesty have everything in common.

If the search yields more results than I can handle should I call that loneliness.

Or lucidity.

If yields no results, modesty?

. . .

The moral anthropology in me dictates: I am mostly looking around outside.

But then there is the question: WHAT IS SLIPPING AWAY FROM WHAT.

(If I slip at least let me be indulgent. Let me look around inside.)

. . .

The crooked caw of first person present.

NINE. **BIRTHDAY NOTEBOOK**

A Canon...is an imaginarie rule, drawing that part of the
Song which is not set downe out of that part which is set
downe. Or it is a Rule, which doth wittily discouer the
secret of a Song.

John Dowland

Today: deep in the Goldberg Variations, Glenn Gould's 1955
recordings.

It is a way to wake into the full white and black keys of the day.

Lie in the white bed.

Lie with the white curtains closed.

. . .

November. A Friday. And look at the body you have.

. . .

It is this whitening skin I am growing old into.

Blackening hair, two white hairs in the beard, the white aria of age, infinite shades of white.

. . .

Today: to note every white note.

Today: to try to whiten all the others.

To see what large thing I may fend off.

. . .

Glenn Gould's teacher developed a way of tapping the keys to fully note every note, regardless of tempo or ordinary dexterous limitations.

This seems like a crucial enough pursuit.

. . .

Glenn Gould hummed along to his playing causing recording disturbances.

What the music contained, the piano alone could not fill.

He could not not fill the notes before him: this is what humming is.

. . .

One hums when one is assuring their partner, mm hmm.

One hums when if one were a chicken it would cluck (contact call).

One hums when one's note must be nasal.

One hums when one is generally feeling well.

One hums out of tune and can generally upset the listener.

One hums when one is bored.

When is booed.

Machines hum.

Insects in flight hum.

Active volcanoes are known to hum, the low frequency audible to some, the same as some knees ache in advance of a rain, a phenomenon I somewhat envy.

Glenn Gould hums.

. . .

Humming along to the primary actions of life (they occur constantly and before you) is the first deluge, and largely a pleasure deluge.

. . .

Yesterday was Thanksgiving and the day before that my lover who assured me she was going to her parents' house without her husband caved into his pleas and the two of them on that car ride caused me to at last shed my faith in the primacy of our affair.

It should sound so easy.

I will continue to pursue her because I am weak, though now both she and I know the peak of our capacity to care for each other is behind us, and I guess we are preparing to discover a beauty in that.

. . .

Another hum, love, would disgrace mankind.

. . .

An involuntary receptacle is the disgraced.

. . .

It is your birthday today, love.

Two feet high and rising.

You are 27 years old, and here I could note anything about
the feelings of maturity, or some charming thing about the
sexual peak, or fallacy, or the ever-humming existential crisis
occurring, or my plans to take you hiking up Mt. Greylock, but
let's face it, anyone at your age can fall in love, but without the
resolve to do anything about it, all of our shared experiences
now are want to collapse into an intimate and hidden-from-you
nook of my heart to be cracked open and sniffed during the
meeting of other lovers I will have.

It has been two days since the crown of my disappointment
in you and already my new and first secrets from you are as
delicious to me as the geese watching when we met.

. . .

My first scents from you.

. . .

Three feet high and rising.

. . .

Today you are not the next theme come true.

I cannot protect you.

I cannot fight flight into the final thought I have tonight, either.
I cannot protect you and I cannot spare myself of you.

. . .

From the heavenly gift of bitter co-loathe.

. . .

I cannot be but canon here.

The follower following first in unison: "Today you are not the
next theme come true."

Tomorrow following in a major second higher than the leader:
"Today you come with your hands in my hair."

. . .

The third day, disaster: "Today come true, you are mere and low and lowly next to the theme of *I am coming.*"

. . .

On the fourth day, the follower begins inverted in the second bar.

So that when you sing, "My love, I thought of you, without you, the entire time we were away," I sing, "Go away. The entire time, I thought of lone love."

. . .

So that when you sing anything, I canonize, "Etcetera." "Etcetera."

. . .

The ways I know that you are not moved by my anguish to treat me better are the same ways I do not feel shame anymore for these matters I speak of here.

. . .

I wonder if H.D. sent you to "go to the under-world or the

gate of heaven, while I tread an earth, devoid of your touch (unutterable bliss), thank God, devoid of your kiss."

. . .

I wonder if you believe me, that I am willing to endure your absence for you, as I no longer want to believe it myself.

. . .

I believe in you so few hours of the day today. The strength of those hours alone binding me to bid more days of enduring for you.

. . .

I wonder what you'd do to me if I didn't bow before you.

Would you still keel white and kiss me.

Would you permit your blue blood to get oxygen red for me.

Would you have me, the monster I am becoming before you.

. . .

I have so many of your hairpins around my apartment, how am I supposed to believe any of them are meaningful.

. . .

How many feet high and rising.

. . .

What worth would you make of me, given a chance to fight for me.

. . .

When we sat in my office and you held your hand on my neck and I closed my eyes, I was picturing you; what will I picture next time you try to breathe safe tremble into me, and will my faith in you be mere and chemical.

. . .

This, my little book, I make for you, can never be white as first snow, which is now falling outside.

I shall go out and touch it.

TEN. **TERMINUS**

Yes you are strong not to touch me.

Strong not to reach even.

I'd like to do one thing on this side of the thing we have, we still have together, if you will.

This thing the nearest side of heaven.

Nearest little heaven.

. . .

I would like to say I would like to steer a little more next time.

. . .

I am okay, steering clouds to heaven.

. . .

I have watched the snow become rain on my chest as the children continue to worry for their bearded neighbor, as children do.

. . .

Maybe all this ever amounts to: the flailing naming, the occasion of ripcord.

Or the opposites of these.

And the words I did not find what I was.

ABOUT THE AUTHOR

DAVID BARTONE'S poems have appeared in *Colorado Review, Denver Quarterly, The Laurel Review, Mountain Gazette, Verse Online,* and others. He is the author of *Spring Logic,* a chapbook with H_NGM_N. He received his MFA from the Program for Poets and Writers at UMass Amherst. He is faculty at University Without Walls at UMass Amherst and lives in Easthampton, MA.

AHSAHTA PRESS

SAWTOOTH POETRY PRIZE SERIES

2002: Aaron McCollough, *Welkin* (Brenda Hillman, judge)

2003: Graham Foust, *Leave the Room to Itself* (Joe Wenderoth, judge)

2004: Noah Eli Gordon, *The Area of Sound Called the Subtone* (Claudia Rankine, judge)

2005: Karla Kelsey, *Knowledge, Forms, The Aviary* (Carolyn Forché, judge)

2006: Paige Ackerson-Kiely, *In No One's Land* (D. A. Powell, judge)

2007: Rusty Morrison, *the true keeps calm biding its story* (Peter Gizzi, judge)

2008: Barbara Maloutas, *the whole Marie* (C. D. Wright, judge)

2009: Julie Carr, *100 Notes on Violence* (Rae Armantrout, judge)

2010: James Meetze, *Dayglo* (Terrance Hayes, judge)

2011: Karen Rigby, *Chinoiserie* (Paul Hoover, judge)

2012: T. Zachary Cotler, *Sonnets to the Humans* (Heather McHugh, judge)

2013: David Bartone, *Practice on Mountains* (Dan Beachy-Quick, judge)